Disaster Preparedness Mastery

Expert Tips and Tricks to Survive Natural and Man-Made Catastrophes

Andy Roffe

Disaster Preparedness Mastery

TABLE OF CONTENTS

Chapter 1: Risk Assessment and Planning

Identifying Potential Risks

Understanding the vast array of potential risks that could disrupt your life is the cornerstone of effective disaster preparedness. Whether you live in an area prone to natural disasters or you're concerned about man-made crises, identifying these risks allows you to develop a strategic plan to mitigate them. This process involves a detailed examination of your environment, lifestyle, and potential threats that could arise. By being proactive, you can significantly reduce the impact of these risks on your life and ensure the safety and well-being of your family.

The first step in identifying potential risks is to conduct a thorough assessment of your geographical location. Different regions are susceptible to different types of natural disasters. If you live along the coast, hurricanes and flooding might be your primary concerns. Inland areas might face tornadoes, severe storms, or droughts. Earthquake-prone regions require specific preparations for seismic activity. Research historical data and consult local authorities to understand the most common and severe risks in your area. This will give you a clear picture of what you need to prepare for.

Next, consider the impact of climate change on your region. Weather patterns are becoming increasingly unpredictable, and areas that were previously safe from certain types of natural disasters may now be at risk. Rising sea levels, increased frequency of wildfires, and more intense storms are just a few examples of how climate change can alter the risk landscape. Stay informed about scientific predictions and updates specific to your location to ensure your preparedness plans remain relevant and effective.

In addition to natural disasters, it's crucial to consider man-made risks. These include industrial accidents, chemical spills, power outages, and even terrorist attacks. Urban areas are particularly vulnerable to such incidents due to the high concentration of people and infrastructure. If you live near a major industrial site, power plant, or transportation hub, familiarize yourself with the types of hazards associated with these facilities. Understand the safety protocols in place and how they might affect you in the event of an emergency.

Technological risks are another significant category to consider. In our increasingly digital world, cyber-attacks and data breaches pose substantial threats. These incidents can disrupt critical services, compromise personal information, and even impact physical infrastructure. Ensure that your digital life is secure by using strong passwords, keeping software up to date, and being aware of the latest cyber threats. Also, consider how a technology failure, like a prolonged internet or power outage, could affect your daily life and prepare accordingly.

Health-related risks should not be overlooked, especially in the wake of recent global pandemics. Infectious diseases can spread rapidly and have devastating effects on communities. Stay informed about potential health threats and ensure you have access to necessary medical supplies and information. Regularly update your vaccinations and have a plan for accessing healthcare during an outbreak. Understanding the specific health risks in your area, such as prevalent diseases or potential exposure to hazardous materials, can also help you prepare more effectively.

Economic risks also play a critical role in disaster preparedness. Financial stability can be severely impacted by both natural and man-made disasters. Job loss, inflation, and market fluctuations can all affect your ability to respond to and recover from a crisis. Building an emergency fund, diversifying your income sources, and having a plan for financial recovery are essential components of comprehensive risk management. Consider the economic implications of different types of disasters and how they might affect your livelihood.

Community-specific risks should also be evaluated. Every community has unique vulnerabilities based on its demographics, infrastructure, and resources. For example, communities with a high population of elderly individuals may face greater challenges during evacuations. Areas with limited access to healthcare facilities or emergency services might struggle more in a crisis. Engage with local community leaders and organizations to understand these specific risks and collaborate on strategies to address them. This community-based approach ensures that your preparedness efforts are aligned with the needs and capabilities of those around you.

Personal lifestyle factors can also influence the types of risks you face. Your daily routines, work environment, and family dynamics all play a role in determining your vulnerability to different hazards. For instance, if you work in a high-rise building, fire safety and evacuation procedures are critical considerations. Families with young children or pets will need to account for their specific needs in any emergency plan. Assess how your lifestyle choices increase or mitigate certain risks and tailor your preparedness efforts accordingly.

To effectively identify potential risks, it's essential to engage in continuous learning and adaptation. Stay updated on the latest research, technologies, and best practices in disaster preparedness. Attend workshops, participate in training exercises, and connect with experts in the field. This ongoing education will help you refine your risk assessment and ensure that your preparedness plans remain robust and relevant.

Another important aspect of risk identification is communication. Share your findings and plans with family members, friends, and neighbors. Open discussions about potential risks and preparedness strategies can foster a culture of awareness and cooperation. Everyone in your household should understand the various risks you face and know their roles in the event of an emergency. This collaborative approach not only enhances individual preparedness but also strengthens community resilience.

Documenting your risk assessment is a crucial step in the process. Create detailed records of the potential risks you've identified, along with the specific actions needed to mitigate them. This documentation should include emergency contact information, evacuation routes, and resource lists. Regularly review and update these documents to reflect any changes in your circumstances or the risk landscape. Having this information readily available ensures that you can act quickly and efficiently when a disaster strikes.

Finally, practice is essential for effective risk management. Conduct regular drills and simulations to test your preparedness plans and identify any gaps or weaknesses. These exercises should cover a range of scenarios, from natural disasters to cyber-attacks, and involve all members of your household. Practicing your response procedures helps to build muscle memory and ensures that everyone knows what to do in an emergency. It also provides an opportunity to refine your plans and improve your overall preparedness.

By systematically identifying potential risks and taking proactive steps to address them, you can significantly enhance your resilience to disasters. This comprehensive approach ensures that you are well-prepared for a wide range of scenarios, reducing the impact on your life and increasing your ability to recover swiftly. Remember, the key to effective disaster preparedness is not just having a plan, but continuously adapting and improving it based on the evolving risk landscape. Stay informed, stay engaged, and stay prepared.

Every household and community has unique vulnerabilities that can amplify the impact of disasters. Analyzing these vulnerabilities is a critical step in disaster preparedness, as it allows you to address weak points and build resilience against potential threats. This chapter delves into the various dimensions of vulnerability, offering practical and actionable advice to fortify your defenses.

Start by assessing the structural integrity of your home. Older buildings, for example, may not be built to withstand modern risks such as severe weather events or earthquakes. Examine the materials used in your home's construction and consider consulting a structural engineer to identify weaknesses. Reinforcing your home might involve retrofitting for seismic activity, installing storm shutters, or upgrading roofing materials to withstand high winds. These improvements, though potentially costly, are invaluable investments in safety.

Next, evaluate the geographical vulnerabilities specific to your location. Living in a floodplain, near a fault line, or in a wildfire-prone area necessitates tailored preparedness measures. For instance, if you reside in a flood-prone area, flood-proofing your home by elevating electrical systems and installing sump pumps can mitigate water damage. Similarly, clearing vegetation and creating defensible space around your property can reduce wildfire risk. Understanding the specific environmental challenges of your region enables you to take targeted actions to safeguard your home and loved ones.

Personal and family vulnerabilities should also be considered. Each household member's age, health, and mobility can affect your overall preparedness. Families with young children need to account for their specific needs, such as baby formula, diapers, and comfort items, in an emergency kit. Elderly family members or those with chronic illnesses may require additional medical supplies, mobility aids, and access to uninterrupted power for medical devices. Creating a personalized emergency plan that addresses these unique needs ensures that everyone in your household is prepared and protected.

Financial vulnerabilities play a significant role in disaster preparedness. Economic stability can be disrupted by both the immediate aftermath and the long-term consequences of a disaster. Assess your financial health by evaluating your savings, insurance coverage, and income stability. Building an emergency fund that covers at least three to six months of living expenses can provide a crucial financial buffer. Additionally, review your insurance policies to ensure they cover the types of disasters most likely to affect your area. Adequate coverage for home, health, and life insurance can significantly ease the financial burden during recovery.

Community vulnerabilities are another critical factor. The resilience of your broader community directly impacts your own preparedness. Engage with local emergency services, neighborhood associations, and community groups to understand the collective vulnerabilities and resources. Participating in community preparedness initiatives, such as neighborhood watch programs or community emergency response teams (CERT), can enhance overall resilience. These groups often provide valuable training and resources, fostering a network of support that can be crucial during a disaster.

Technological vulnerabilities have become increasingly relevant in our digital age. Power outages, cyber-attacks, and communications breakdowns can severely disrupt your ability to respond to and recover from a disaster. Ensure you have backup power solutions, such as generators or solar chargers, to keep essential devices running. Protect your digital information by regularly backing up important files and using strong, unique passwords for online accounts. Consider how a prolonged loss of internet or mobile service would affect your daily life and develop contingency plans for staying informed and connected.

Health vulnerabilities extend beyond immediate medical needs to include mental health considerations. Disasters can cause significant stress, anxiety, and trauma, affecting your ability to respond effectively. Incorporate mental health strategies into your preparedness plan by identifying coping mechanisms, such as mindfulness practices or physical exercise, that work for you. Maintain a list of mental health resources, including crisis hotlines and local support services, to access if needed.

Prioritizing mental well-being ensures you remain resilient and capable during challenging times.

Transportation vulnerabilities are another aspect to consider. Assess your reliance on personal and public transportation and plan for scenarios where these might be unavailable. Ensure your vehicle is well-maintained and always has a full tank of gas. Keep a portable emergency kit in your car, including essentials like water, non-perishable food, blankets, and a first aid kit. If you rely on public transportation, identify alternative routes and backup options for getting to safety. Additionally, consider the needs of those without access to personal transportation and how you might assist them during an evacuation.

Communication vulnerabilities can hinder your ability to stay informed and coordinate with others. Establish a communication plan that includes multiple methods of staying in touch, such as phone calls, text messages, and social media. Ensure everyone in your household knows the plan and has access to necessary contact information. Consider investing in a battery-powered or hand-crank radio to receive emergency broadcasts if electronic communication fails. Having a plan in place to relay information and updates can reduce confusion and stress during a crisis.

Finally, consider the temporal vulnerabilities that arise from the timing of a disaster. Disasters can strike at any time, often with little warning. Prepare for various scenarios, including those that occur during the night, while at work or school, or when key family members are away. Develop flexible plans that account for different times of day and circumstances, ensuring that everyone knows their responsibilities and actions regardless of when a disaster occurs. Regular drills and practice runs can help solidify these plans and increase your readiness.

By thoroughly analyzing and addressing these vulnerabilities, you build a robust foundation for disaster preparedness. This proactive approach not only minimizes the risks but also enhances your ability to respond swiftly and effectively when disaster strikes. Remember, preparedness is an ongoing process that requires regular reassessment and adaptation. Stay vigilant, stay informed, and continuously refine your strategies to ensure you and your loved ones remain safe and resilient in the face of adversity.

Creating a disaster plan is essential for ensuring that you and your loved ones can navigate emergencies with confidence and efficiency. This chapter will guide you through the steps of crafting a comprehensive disaster plan that is tailored to your unique circumstances and risks.

Begin by gathering your family or household members to discuss the importance of having a disaster plan. This initial meeting sets the tone and ensures that everyone understands their role in the event of an emergency. Open communication is key, so encourage questions and suggestions from all participants. Start by identifying the types of disasters that are most likely to affect your area, such as hurricanes, earthquakes, floods, or wildfires. Understanding the specific threats you face will inform the details of your plan.

Next, establish clear and concise communication strategies. Determine how you will contact each other during an emergency if regular communication channels are disrupted. Consider using a combination of methods, such as phone calls, text messages, emails, and social media. Designate a primary and secondary meeting place where everyone can gather if evacuation is necessary. It's also prudent to identify an out-of-town contact person who can act as a liaison for your family, helping to relay information if local lines are down.

Develop an evacuation plan that includes several routes and modes of transportation. Familiarize yourself with local evacuation routes and shelters, and ensure that all family members know how to get there. Practice these routes regularly to build familiarity and confidence. If you have pets, make sure your plan includes provisions for their safe evacuation as well. Keep a carrier or leash handy and ensure that your pets' identification tags are up to date.

Create a detailed emergency kit that contains all the essentials you might need during a disaster. This kit should include water, non-perishable food, a first aid kit, medications, flashlights, batteries, a multi-tool, important documents, and cash. Customize the contents based on the specific needs of your family, such as baby supplies, pet food, and extra glasses or contact lenses. Store your kit in a readily accessible location and check it regularly to replace expired items and update its contents.

Consider the unique needs of each family member when crafting your plan. Children, elderly relatives, and individuals with disabilities may require additional assistance and resources. Ensure that your plan addresses these needs comprehensively. For example, if you have a family member with mobility issues, identify evacuation methods and routes that accommodate their limitations. Keep a supply of necessary medical equipment and medications, and have a backup power source for medical devices if required.

Incorporate health and hygiene considerations into your disaster plan. Include items such as hand sanitizers, masks, and sanitary wipes in your emergency kit to maintain cleanliness and prevent the spread of illness. Understand the potential health risks associated with different types of disasters and prepare accordingly. For example, floodwaters can carry contaminants, so having water purification tablets or a portable water filter can be crucial.

Financial preparedness is another critical aspect of your disaster plan. Ensure that you have access to funds in an emergency by keeping some cash on hand, as electronic payment systems may be down. Review your insurance policies to confirm that you have adequate coverage for the types of disasters you are most likely to encounter. Keep copies of important financial documents, such as insurance policies, bank account information, and identification, in a waterproof and fireproof container. Consider setting up an emergency fund to cover unexpected expenses during and after a disaster.

Regularly review and practice your disaster plan to ensure that everyone knows their roles and responsibilities. Conduct drills that simulate different scenarios, such as evacuating the house in case of a fire or sheltering in place during a storm. These exercises help to identify any gaps or weaknesses in your plan and provide an opportunity to refine your strategies. Encourage feedback from all participants and make adjustments as needed to improve the plan's effectiveness.

Stay informed about potential threats by signing up for local emergency alerts and monitoring weather reports. Many communities offer alert systems that can send notifications via text message or email about imminent threats and evacuation orders. Familiarize yourself with the different types of alerts and what actions you should take when you receive them. Being informed allows you to act quickly and make informed decisions during an emergency.

Incorporate community resources into your disaster plan. Identify local shelters, food banks, and medical facilities that can provide assistance during a disaster. Establish connections with neighbors and community organizations to create a support network. Knowing that you have a broader support system can provide peace of mind and additional resources in times of need.

Finally, consider the long-term aspects of disaster preparedness. Develop a recovery plan that outlines the steps you will take to rebuild and return to normalcy after a disaster. This plan should include contacting insurance providers, assessing property damage, and accessing community resources for assistance. Having a clear recovery plan can help to reduce stress and expedite the process of getting back on your feet.

Creating a disaster plan is a dynamic process that requires regular updates and adjustments. As your family grows and circumstances change, revisit your plan to ensure it remains relevant and effective. Continuous improvement and practice are key to maintaining a state of readiness. By taking these proactive steps, you can safeguard your family and enhance your resilience in the face of adversity. Consider the importance of mental and emotional preparedness as a component of your disaster plan. Disasters can be traumatic and stressful, so it's essential to have strategies in place to cope with these challenges. Discuss with your family the potential emotional impacts of a disaster and create a supportive environment where everyone feels comfortable expressing their fears and concerns. Identify coping mechanisms that work for each family member, such as talking with a trusted friend, engaging in physical activity, or practicing mindfulness and relaxation techniques.

Involving family members in any significant endeavor requires careful consideration and a thoughtful approach. This chapter delves into how to engage your family effectively, ensuring that each member is both invested in and contributes to the collective goals.

Start by acknowledging the unique dynamics of your family. Each family member brings different strengths, weaknesses, and perspectives to the table. Recognizing and valuing these individual differences is crucial for fostering a collaborative environment. Begin with an open discussion where everyone can express their thoughts and feelings about the project or goal at hand. This initial conversation sets the stage for mutual understanding and respect, which are foundational to any successful family collaboration.

Establish clear and shared goals to give everyone a sense of purpose and direction. When setting these goals, involve all family members in the decision-making process to ensure that everyone feels a sense of ownership. This inclusiveness not only boosts motivation but also fosters a sense of responsibility. Discuss what success looks like and outline the steps needed to achieve it. Having a clear roadmap helps each person understand their role and how their contributions fit into the bigger picture.

Communication is the cornerstone of effective family involvement. Regular family meetings can be an excellent forum for discussing progress, addressing concerns, and making necessary adjustments to your plans. These meetings should be structured yet flexible, allowing for both formal updates and informal conversations. Encourage open and honest communication, where everyone feels safe to voice their opinions and ideas. Active listening is key—ensure that each person feels heard and understood.

Assign roles and responsibilities based on individual strengths and interests. This strategy not only ensures that tasks are completed efficiently but also helps each family member feel valued and engaged. For example, if one member is particularly good with numbers, they might handle budgeting or financial planning. Another might excel in organizing and could take on logistical aspects. By leveraging each person's unique skills, you create a more effective and harmonious team.

Flexibility and adaptability are essential qualities when involving family members. Life is unpredictable, and circumstances can change rapidly. Be prepared to adjust your plans and strategies as needed. This might mean redistributing tasks, extending deadlines, or finding new ways to motivate and engage family members. Flexibility ensures that the family can navigate challenges without becoming discouraged or disheartened.

Celebrate successes, both big and small, to maintain morale and motivation. Recognizing and rewarding achievements fosters a positive atmosphere and encourages continued effort. Celebrations can be simple, such as a special family dinner or a small token of appreciation. The key is to show gratitude and acknowledge the hard work and contributions of each family member.

Education and skill development should also be a part of your strategy. Providing opportunities for family members to learn and grow not only enhances their ability to contribute but also shows that you value their personal development. This could involve formal training, workshops, or even just sharing relevant resources and information. Encouraging a culture of continuous learning benefits the family as a whole and helps each person reach their full potential.

Conflict is inevitable in any group effort, and how you handle it can make or break the success of your family's endeavors. Address conflicts promptly and constructively, focusing on resolving issues rather than assigning blame. Use conflicts as opportunities for growth and learning. Encourage family members to express their feelings and work together to find mutually acceptable solutions. Effective conflict resolution strengthens relationships and builds a more resilient family unit.

Empathy and understanding are critical when involving family members. Each person's life experiences, personality, and current circumstances influence how they perceive and react to situations. Strive to see things from their perspective and show compassion for their challenges and concerns. This empathetic approach fosters a supportive environment where everyone feels valued and respected.

Transparency in decision-making and progress updates builds trust and accountability. Keep everyone informed about the status of the project, any changes to plans, and the rationale behind decisions. This openness helps to avoid misunderstandings and ensures that everyone is on the same page. When family members understand the bigger picture, they are more likely to stay committed and motivated.

Creating a supportive environment extends beyond the immediate project or goal. Foster a family culture that values cooperation, mutual support, and shared responsibility in all aspects of life. Encourage family members to help each other with personal challenges and celebrate each other's achievements. This holistic approach strengthens the family bond and creates a solid foundation for any collective endeavor.

Encourage and model resilience in the face of setbacks and failures. Every journey has its ups and downs, and how you respond to challenges sets the tone for the entire family. Demonstrate perseverance and a positive attitude, and encourage family members to view obstacles as opportunities for learning and growth. Resilience helps the family stay united and focused on their goals, even when things don't go as planned.

Lastly, ensure that the involvement of family members is balanced with their individual needs and commitments. Respect each person's time and energy, and avoid overburdening them with responsibilities. Strive for a balance that allows everyone to contribute meaningfully while still attending to their personal lives and well-being. This balance is crucial for maintaining long-term engagement and avoiding burnout.

In conclusion, involving family members in any significant endeavor requires a thoughtful and strategic approach. By fostering open communication, recognizing individual strengths, being flexible, and maintaining a supportive environment, you can create a collaborative and motivated family team. Celebrating successes, addressing conflicts constructively, and encouraging continuous learning further strengthen the family's ability to work together effectively. Through empathy, transparency, and resilience, you can navigate challenges and achieve your collective goals while ensuring that each family member feels valued and supported. This comprehensive approach not only enhances the success of your current project but also builds a stronger, more united family for the future.

A comprehensive disaster preparedness plan is not a static document; it requires regular updates to remain effective. Life is dynamic, with changes in family circumstances, evolving threats, and technological advancements necessitating continual revisions. Regularly updating your plan ensures it remains relevant and actionable when you need it most.

Begin by scheduling regular reviews of your disaster preparedness plan. Set a routine, such as quarterly or bi-annual evaluations, to systematically go through every aspect of your plan. These scheduled reviews should be as non-negotiable as any other critical appointment in your calendar. Regular reviews help you stay proactive, allowing you to identify and address potential issues before they become significant problems.

During each review, start by examining any changes in your family's circumstances. This includes but is not limited to new additions to the family, changes in medical conditions, or shifts in living arrangements. For instance, if a new baby has arrived, you'll need to consider additional supplies and special needs. If an elderly family member moves in, mobility and medical support considerations must be updated. These personal changes can significantly impact your preparedness strategy, requiring adjustments in emergency supplies, evacuation plans, and communication strategies.

Next, assess the current state of local and regional threats. Natural disasters, such as hurricanes, earthquakes, floods, and wildfires, can vary in frequency and intensity over time. Additionally, man-made threats like industrial accidents or changes in crime rates can alter the risk landscape. Keep abreast of updates from local emergency management agencies and incorporate any new information into your plan. This might involve updating evacuation routes or identifying new safe locations.

Technology evolves rapidly, offering new tools and resources for disaster preparedness. Review and integrate new apps, devices, and systems that can enhance your plan. For example, new weather alert systems, advanced home security features, or updated emergency communication tools can provide better information and coordination during a disaster. Staying current with technological advancements ensures that you leverage the best available tools to keep your family safe.

Inventory management is another critical aspect of regularly updating your plan. Emergency supplies can degrade or become obsolete over time. Conduct regular checks of your emergency kits, ensuring that food, water, batteries, medications, and other essentials are within their expiration dates and in good condition. Replace any items that are expired or damaged. Keeping an updated inventory list can streamline this process, making it easier to track what needs replenishing.

Communication plans should also be revisited regularly. Ensure that contact information for all family members, friends, and emergency contacts is current. This includes phone numbers, email addresses, and social media handles. Practice your communication plan periodically to ensure everyone knows how to reach each other during an emergency. This practice can reveal any gaps or issues in your plan, allowing you to address them before a real disaster occurs.

Review and update your financial preparedness as well. This includes ensuring that you have access to emergency funds and that important financial documents are current and accessible. Consider changes in your financial situation, such as new insurance policies, loans, or major purchases, and how they might affect your preparedness. Keeping financial information up-to-date is crucial for a smooth recovery process after a disaster.

Training and education are ongoing components of disaster preparedness. Regularly update and expand the knowledge and skills of all family members. This might include first aid training, CPR certification, or learning how to use new emergency equipment. Encourage participation in community preparedness programs and drills. Keeping skills sharp and knowledge current ensures that everyone is prepared to act effectively in an emergency.

Regularly updating your plan also involves revisiting your evacuation procedures. Changes in infrastructure, construction, and traffic patterns can affect the best routes and methods for evacuating your area. Ensure that your evacuation routes are still viable and that everyone in the family is familiar with them. Practice evacuation drills to reinforce this knowledge and identify any potential issues.

A crucial part of updating your plan is learning from past experiences. If you have faced a disaster or participated in a drill, review what went well and what did not. Use these insights to refine your plan. This reflective process helps you build on successes and address weaknesses, making your plan more robust over time.

Engaging with your community is another important aspect of regularly updating your plan. Stay connected with local emergency management agencies, community groups, and neighbors. Participate in community meetings and preparedness activities. Sharing information and resources with your community can enhance your overall preparedness and provide additional support networks.

Finally, document all updates and changes to your plan clearly and concisely. Maintain both digital and hard copies of the updated plan, and ensure that all family members have access to the latest version. Clear documentation helps avoid confusion and ensures that everyone is informed about the current procedures and protocols.

In summary, regularly updating your disaster preparedness plan is a dynamic and ongoing process. By scheduling regular reviews, assessing changes in personal circumstances and local threats, integrating new technology, managing inventory, revisiting communication and evacuation plans, keeping financial information current, maintaining training, learning from past experiences, engaging with the community, and documenting updates, you can ensure that your plan remains effective and actionable. This proactive approach not only enhances your readiness but also provides peace of mind, knowing that you and your family are prepared for whatever challenges may arise.

Chapter 2: Building a Comprehensive Emergency Kit

Essential Supplies

When preparing for any disaster, having the right supplies can make all the difference in ensuring safety, comfort, and survival. Essential supplies are the backbone of disaster preparedness, providing the necessary resources to navigate through emergencies with confidence and resilience. This chapter outlines the critical items every household should stockpile, offering practical advice on how to gather, maintain, and effectively use these supplies.

Start by focusing on the most fundamental need: water. Water is vital for drinking, cooking, and hygiene. Each person in your household requires at least one gallon of water per day, with a recommended stockpile for a minimum of three days, though having a two-week supply is ideal. Store water in clean, food-grade containers, and consider water purification options such as portable filters, purification tablets, or household bleach. Rotate your water supply every six months to ensure freshness.

Food supplies are equally crucial. Aim to stockpile non-perishable items that are easy to prepare and have a long shelf life. Canned goods, dried fruits, nuts, peanut butter, and shelf-stable milk are excellent choices. Include comfort foods like chocolate or coffee to help maintain morale during stressful times. Ensure you have a manual can opener, as power outages may render electric ones useless. Pay attention to any dietary restrictions or allergies within the household, and include baby food or formula if necessary.

Medical supplies are essential for treating injuries and managing health conditions during a disaster. A well-stocked first aid kit should include bandages, antiseptics, pain relievers, scissors, tweezers, and medical gloves. Additionally, ensure you have an adequate supply of prescription medications, over-the-counter drugs, and any necessary medical equipment such as inhalers, blood glucose meters, or spare eyeglasses. Regularly check expiration dates and replace items as needed.

Shelter and warmth are vital, especially in the event of power outages or evacuation. Blankets, sleeping bags, and warm clothing can protect against the cold. Consider including a tent or tarps with duct tape to create makeshift shelters if needed. Ponchos, raincoats, and sturdy footwear will help you stay dry and protected in adverse weather conditions. Hand warmers and emergency blankets, which are compact and efficient, can also provide essential warmth.

Hygiene and sanitation supplies are often overlooked but are critical in preventing illness and maintaining dignity during a disaster. Stock up on soap, hand sanitizer, toilet paper, moist towelettes, and garbage bags with ties. Include feminine hygiene products, diapers for infants, and any other specific needs for family members. Portable toilets or buckets with tight-fitting lids can serve as emergency sanitation solutions if regular facilities are unavailable.

Tools and equipment play an indispensable role in disaster preparedness. A multi-tool, flashlight, batteries, matches, and a portable stove or grill are invaluable. Solar chargers or power banks can keep essential electronics operational. Keep a supply of sturdy plastic bags, duct tape, and basic repair tools like hammers and screwdrivers to address minor damages or create makeshift solutions. Ensure your toolkit is readily accessible and that everyone in the household knows how to use the items within it.

Communication is critical during any emergency. A battery-powered or hand-crank radio can provide crucial updates and information when other communication channels fail. Keep a list of emergency contact numbers and a charged mobile phone with backup batteries or a solar charger. Walkie-talkies can be beneficial for short-range communication, particularly if family members are separated.

Financial preparedness is another key aspect to consider. Keep a stash of cash in small denominations, as ATMs and credit card machines may not work during power outages. Important documents such as identification, insurance policies, and medical records should be stored in a waterproof, portable container. Having these documents readily accessible can expedite recovery and aid in accessing necessary services.

Personal safety should not be neglected. Basic self-defense items, such as pepper spray or a whistle, can provide a sense of security. Reflective clothing or vests ensure visibility in low-light conditions, reducing the risk of accidents. Familiarize all family members with the location and proper use of these safety items.

Pet supplies are often forgotten but are crucial for households with animals. Ensure you have enough food, water, and any necessary medications for your pets. Include items like leashes, carriers, and comfort items such as blankets or toys. A photo of your pet and copies of their medical records can be helpful if you become separated.

Entertainment and comfort items can greatly improve morale during stressful times. Books, playing cards, board games, and puzzles can provide much-needed distractions. Consider including items that are soothing or comforting, like favorite snacks, a journal, or a cherished blanket.

Once you have gathered your essential supplies, organize them in an easily accessible location. Store items in labeled, waterproof containers, and keep your emergency kit in a designated spot known to all household members. Regularly review and update your supplies, replacing expired items and adjusting the contents based on seasonal changes or evolving family needs.

Engage all family members in the process of gathering and maintaining these supplies. Assign specific responsibilities to each person, ensuring everyone understands the importance of their role. Practice using the supplies and conduct regular drills to reinforce familiarity and readiness.

In conclusion, essential supplies are the cornerstone of any disaster preparedness plan. By ensuring you have adequate water, food, medical supplies, shelter, hygiene items, tools, communication devices, financial resources, safety equipment, pet supplies, and entertainment options, you can provide for your family's needs during an emergency. Regularly reviewing and updating these supplies, and involving all family members in the process, ensures that your household is well-prepared to face any disaster with confidence and resilience.

Preparing for different types of disasters requires a tailored approach, as each scenario demands unique supplies and strategies. Understanding the specific needs for various emergencies ensures that your preparedness plan is both comprehensive and effective. This chapter delves into the specialized items necessary for a range of disasters, from natural events like hurricanes and earthquakes to man-made crises such as chemical spills and power outages.

For hurricanes, having sturdy, waterproof containers for your essentials is crucial. These storms bring heavy rain and flooding, so keeping your supplies dry is a priority. An emergency weather radio, preferably hand-crank or battery-powered, provides critical updates as the storm progresses. Tarps and plastic sheeting can be used to cover windows or create temporary shelter if your home is damaged. Additionally, a supply of sandbags can help protect your property from floodwaters. Ensure you have a whistle to signal for help if you are trapped by debris or rising water.

Earthquakes demand a focus on safety and rapid response. Your emergency kit should include a pair of sturdy shoes and gloves to protect against broken glass and debris. A crowbar or pry bar can be essential for freeing yourself or others from trapped areas. Secure a supply of dust masks to protect your lungs from dust and debris in the aftermath. Flashlights with extra batteries or glow sticks are vital as power outages are common. Keep a supply of heavy-duty plastic bags for sanitation purposes, as plumbing may be disrupted.

For wildfires, evacuation is often necessary, so your kit should be portable and ready to go at a moment's notice. An N95 mask or a similar respirator is essential to protect against smoke inhalation. Fire-resistant clothing and blankets can provide additional protection. Keep a map with multiple evacuation routes, as fires can change direction rapidly, and roads may become impassable. A portable air purifier can help maintain clean air in your vehicle or temporary shelter. Include goggles to protect your eyes from smoke and embers.

Floods require a focus on waterproofing and mobility. Waterproof bags or containers are crucial for keeping documents, electronics, and other sensitive items safe. A life jacket for each family member is a prudent addition, especially if you live in an area prone to severe flooding. Inflatable rafts or boats can be lifesavers in extreme situations. Include a supply of water purification tablets or a portable filter, as floodwaters often contaminate drinking water sources. Rubber boots and rain gear help protect against the elements during evacuation or rescue efforts.

Tornadoes necessitate quick sheltering and post-storm recovery. A sturdy helmet or hard hat can protect against flying debris. Keep heavy blankets or sleeping bags within easy reach to cover yourself in case you need to take shelter quickly. A whistle or air horn can help signal rescuers if you are trapped. Post-storm, a chainsaw or handsaw can be invaluable for clearing fallen trees and debris. Ensure you have a supply of tarps and duct tape to make temporary repairs to your home.

For winter storms and extreme cold, focus on warmth and maintaining heat. Blankets, sleeping bags rated for low temperatures, and thermal underwear are essential. Battery-powered hand warmers and chemical heat packs can provide additional warmth. A supply of rock salt or cat litter helps to melt ice and improve traction on walkways. A snow shovel is necessary for clearing paths and driveways. Keep a supply of non-perishable, easy-to-prepare foods, as power outages can make cooking difficult. A camping stove or portable heater, along with proper ventilation, can provide warmth and cooking capabilities if the power goes out.

Chemical spills and hazardous material incidents require specialized protective gear. A supply of N95 masks or respirators with appropriate filters is crucial. Chemical-resistant gloves, goggles, and coveralls provide additional protection. Sealable plastic bags help contain contaminated clothing and other items. Keep a supply of bottled water and non-perishable food in case of contamination of local resources. An emergency decontamination kit, including soap, water, and towels, can be used to clean exposed skin and prevent further exposure.

Power outages, while often a secondary effect of other disasters, require their own set of specialized items. A generator can keep essential appliances running, but ensure you have fuel stored safely. Solar chargers or power banks can keep phones and small electronics charged. Battery-powered fans and heaters help maintain comfort in extreme temperatures. Keep a supply of glow sticks and candles, but use caution with open flames. A manual can opener is essential for accessing canned food.

Pandemics and biological threats necessitate a focus on hygiene and medical supplies. A supply of masks, gloves, and hand sanitizer is essential. Over-the-counter medications, such as fever reducers and cough suppressants, help manage symptoms. A thermometer allows you to monitor for fevers. Keep a supply of non-perishable food and water to minimize trips outside. Soap and disinfectants help maintain cleanliness and reduce the risk of infection. Consider a pulse oximeter to monitor oxygen levels if respiratory issues arise.

Terrorist attacks and civil unrest require a focus on security and communication. A supply of first aid items specifically for treating trauma, such as tourniquets and clotting agents, is crucial. An emergency radio keeps you informed of ongoing threats and evacuation orders. Consider a personal safety alarm to alert authorities if you are in danger. Keep important documents and cash in a secure, portable container. A sturdy pair of shoes and clothing that allows for quick movement can be vital if you need to evacuate quickly.

In each of these scenarios, having a well-thought-out plan and specialized items tailored to the specific disaster can greatly increase your chances of staying safe and managing the situation effectively. Regularly review and update your supplies, considering the unique risks in your area and the specific needs of your household. By preparing for the particular challenges of different disasters, you ensure that you are ready to respond with confidence and resilience.

Customizing Kits for Individual Needs

Disaster preparedness is not a one-size-fits-all endeavor. Each family or individual has unique needs that must be considered when assembling an emergency kit. Customizing your kit ensures that all members of your household, including pets, are adequately prepared for any situation. This chapter will guide you through the process of tailoring your emergency supplies to meet specific requirements, from medical needs to dietary restrictions, ensuring that your kit is comprehensive and effective.

Begin by assessing the medical needs of each family member. If someone in your household has a chronic condition, such as diabetes or heart disease, your kit should include a sufficient supply of their medications, along with any necessary medical equipment like insulin pumps or blood pressure monitors. It's wise to keep an extra pair of eyeglasses or contact lenses and supplies in your kit as well. For those with severe allergies, ensure you have an EpiPen or similar epinephrine injector on hand. Regularly check expiration dates and rotate items as needed to keep your supplies current.

Dietary restrictions and food allergies are critical considerations when customizing your kit. Stock non-perishable foods that cater to these needs, such as gluten-free or dairy-free options. For infants, include formula and baby food that match their dietary requirements. Remember to have a manual can opener if your supplies include canned goods. High-energy snacks like nuts and dried fruits are excellent choices, but always ensure they align with any dietary restrictions in your household. It's also beneficial to include comfort foods that can provide a psychological boost during stressful times.

Pets are an integral part of many families and need to be accounted for in your emergency planning. Create a separate kit for your pets that includes food, water, bowls, leashes, and carriers. Don't forget to pack any medications your pets may require. A familiar toy or blanket can help reduce their stress during an emergency. Keep copies of vaccination records and a recent photo of your pet in your kit, which can be crucial if you become separated. Consider microchipping your pets if you haven't already, as this can greatly increase the chances of being reunited if they get lost.

Children have their own unique needs that should be addressed in your emergency preparations. Infants and toddlers require diapers, wipes, and formula, while older children may need specific medications or comfort items like favorite toys or blankets. Educational and entertainment items such as books, coloring supplies, or small games can help keep children occupied and reduce their anxiety during an emergency. Ensure that your kit includes child-friendly snacks and drinks, as well as basic hygiene supplies tailored for young ones.

Elderly family members may have additional needs that should be considered. Mobility aids like canes, walkers, or wheelchairs should be easily accessible, and your kit should include any hearing aids and extra batteries. Keep a list of medications, dosages, and a schedule, along with a supply of the necessary drugs. If the elderly person has dietary restrictions or needs special nutrition, ensure these are included in your food supplies. An extra blanket or warm clothing can also be crucial, as older adults may be more susceptible to cold.

Individuals with disabilities or special needs require tailored considerations in your emergency kit. This might include specific medical equipment, communication devices, or adapted tools for daily living. For those who rely on electricity for medical devices such as oxygen concentrators or mobility aids, a backup power source like a portable generator or battery pack is essential. Ensure that your kit includes items that support their independence and well-being, such as accessible hygiene products or adaptive utensils.

During emergencies, mental health can be as important as physical health. Incorporate items that support mental well-being, such as stress-relief tools, comfort items, and activities that provide a sense of normalcy. A journal, for instance, can offer an outlet for stress and anxiety. Familiar items like family photos or a cherished book can also provide comfort. If anyone in your household takes medication for mental health conditions, make sure to include a sufficient supply in your kit.

Language barriers can pose a significant challenge during emergencies. For households where English is not the primary language, include translated instructions and important documents in the preferred language. Flashcards or translation apps can be helpful tools for communication. Ensure that everyone understands how to use the items in the emergency kit and can follow the disaster plan. Community resources, such as local support groups or bilingual emergency services, can also be valuable.

Financial preparedness is another critical aspect of a customized emergency kit. Keep cash in small denominations, as ATMs and credit card systems may be down during a disaster. Important documents, including identification, insurance policies, and bank information, should be stored in a waterproof, portable container. Consider making digital copies of these documents and storing them on a secure, password-protected flash drive. This ensures that you have access to essential information even if the physical copies are lost or damaged.

Communication plans are vital for keeping in touch with loved ones during an emergency. Designate an out-of-town contact person who can relay information between separated family members. Ensure that everyone in your household knows this contact's phone number and email address. Include a list of emergency contacts in your kit, along with a battery-powered or hand-crank radio to receive updates. Walkie-talkies can be useful for short-range communication if cell service is unavailable.

Finally, take into account the unique environmental factors relevant to your location. If you live in an area prone to wildfires, include N95 masks to protect against smoke inhalation. For regions susceptible to flooding, ensure that your important documents and electronics are stored in waterproof containers. In areas with extreme cold, prioritize warm clothing, blankets, and a means to generate heat. Tailoring your kit to your specific environment ensures that you are prepared for the most likely scenarios you may face.

Customizing your emergency kit to meet the diverse needs of your household is an ongoing process. Regularly review and update your supplies to account for changing needs, seasonal variations, and new family members. Involve everyone in the household in the planning and preparation process to ensure that all needs and preferences are considered. By taking these steps, you can create a comprehensive and personalized emergency kit that provides security and peace of mind for all members of your household.

Disaster preparedness doesn't end once you've assembled your emergency kit; it's an ongoing process that requires regular maintenance and updates to ensure readiness. A well-maintained kit can make the difference between resilience and vulnerability when disaster strikes. Therefore, this chapter focuses on practical strategies for keeping your emergency supplies in top condition, ensuring they remain effective and reliable.

Start by establishing a routine for checking and maintaining your kit. Set specific dates on your calendar, such as the start of each season, to review your supplies. Seasonal changes often bring different risks and requirements, making these intervals ideal for updates. During these checks, inspect every item in your kit for signs of wear, damage, or expiration. Food, water, medications, and batteries are particularly prone to degradation over time and should be scrutinized closely.

Food and water supplies are essential components of any emergency kit, but they require careful management. Non-perishable foods still have a shelf life, and water stored in plastic containers can develop a stale taste or become contaminated. Rotate your stock by using older items first and replacing them with fresh supplies. This practice, known as FIFO (First In, First Out), ensures that your food and water remain safe and palatable. Consider incorporating high-energy snacks like granola bars and trail mix, which have long shelf lives and provide vital nutrients during emergencies.

Medications are another critical aspect that necessitates regular attention. Prescription drugs, over-the-counter medications, and medical supplies like insulin and inhalers can lose potency or expire. Keep a list of expiration dates and replace items as needed. If someone in your household has a chronic condition, ensure that you have an ample supply of their medications, factoring in potential delays in refilling prescriptions during a disaster. It's also wise to include a copy of each family member's medical information, including allergies, current medications, and doctor contact details.

Batteries and electronic devices require special care to ensure they function when needed. Check batteries in flashlights, radios, and other battery-operated devices regularly, and replace them if they show any signs of leakage or corrosion. Store spare batteries in a cool, dry place to extend their shelf life. For rechargeable devices, make it a habit to fully charge them during your routine checks. Consider investing in a solar charger or hand-crank generator for an alternative power source if the grid goes down.

Clothing and blankets in your emergency kit should be seasonally appropriate and in good condition. Swap out items as needed to reflect the current weather conditions. For example, replace summer clothes with warmer layers and thermal blankets as winter approaches. Ensure that each family member has a complete set of clothing, including sturdy shoes, socks, and undergarments. Waterproof and windproof outerwear can be crucial in protecting against the elements.

Documentation is often overlooked but is vital during emergencies. Keep photocopies of important documents such as identification, insurance policies, bank account details, and medical records in a waterproof container. Regularly review these documents to ensure they are up-to-date and reflect any changes in your circumstances. Consider storing digital copies on a secure, password-protected flash drive for additional backup. Having quick access to these documents can expedite recovery processes and reduce stress during a crisis.

Personal hygiene items, including soap, toothpaste, and sanitary supplies, should be checked for expiration and usability. Replace products that have dried out, leaked, or are nearing their expiration date. Include a sufficient supply of these items to last at least a week, and consider the specific needs of each family member. For instance, include baby wipes and diapers if you have infants or toddlers, and feminine hygiene products if necessary.

Tools and equipment in your emergency kit, such as knives, multi-tools, and cooking gear, should be inspected for functionality. Sharpen blades, lubricate moving parts, and replace any broken or worn-out items. Ensure that you have the means to make basic repairs and adjustments to your kit. Duct tape, sewing kits, and small hand tools can be invaluable for fixing minor issues on the spot.

First aid supplies must be meticulously maintained. Check the contents of your first aid kit for expired items and replenish as needed. Bandages, antiseptic wipes, and adhesive tape can deteriorate over time, so replace them regularly. Include a first aid manual and ensure that all family members know how to use the supplies correctly. Consider enrolling in a first aid course to stay informed about the latest techniques and best practices.

Communication tools, such as radios and cell phones, are crucial for staying informed and connected during a disaster. Test these devices regularly to ensure they are operational. Keep a list of important phone numbers, including emergency services, family members, and neighbors, in both physical and digital formats. Consider adding a whistle or signal flare to your kit for attracting attention if you become trapped or need help.

Customizing your kit to address the unique needs of your household is an essential aspect of maintenance. As family dynamics change, such as the birth of a child or the adoption of a pet, update your supplies accordingly. Regularly review your family's specific requirements and adjust your kit to ensure it remains relevant and comprehensive. This might include adding baby formula, pet food, or specialized medical equipment.

Engaging your entire household in the maintenance process can foster a sense of preparedness and responsibility. Assign tasks to each family member, such as checking expiration dates, testing equipment, or updating documents. Conduct regular drills to ensure everyone knows how to access and use the emergency kit. These exercises can highlight any gaps or areas for improvement in your preparedness plan.

Maintaining a well-equipped emergency kit is not just about replacing expired items or updating supplies. It's also about fostering a mindset of readiness and resilience. Stay informed about potential threats and changes in your local environment. Join community preparedness groups or attend workshops to stay current on best practices. By keeping your kit updated and involving your household in the process, you ensure that you are ready to face any challenge with confidence and calm.

Regular maintenance of your emergency kit is crucial for ensuring its effectiveness. Through diligent checks, updates, and involvement of all family members, you can ensure that your emergency supplies remain reliable and ready for any situation. This proactive approach not only enhances your physical preparedness but also builds a resilient mindset capable of facing any adversity.

Emergencies can strike without warning, leaving little time to gather essential documents and records. Having these critical items organized and readily accessible can significantly streamline recovery efforts, reduce stress, and ensure continuity of care and support. This chapter delves into the importance of maintaining a comprehensive collection of emergency documents and records, providing practical advice on what to include, how to organize them, and strategies for safe storage.

Begin by identifying the most crucial documents that you would need during an emergency. These include personal identification documents such as birth certificates, passports, and driver's licenses. These documents are essential for verifying identity, accessing services, and re-establishing your life post-disaster. Make sure each family member has their own set of identification documents, and consider including copies of Social Security cards as well.

Financial records are another vital category. Gather recent bank statements, credit card information, and mortgage or rental agreements. These documents are necessary for accessing your funds, filing insurance claims, and proving residency. It's also prudent to include information on any loans and debts, such as car payments and student loans. By having these details at hand, you can manage your financial obligations more effectively during a crisis.

Health-related documents are equally important. Create a comprehensive medical file for each family member that includes health insurance cards, a list of current medications and dosages, medical histories, and contact information for primary care physicians and specialists. If anyone in your household has a chronic condition or special needs, ensure that this information is detailed in the medical file. Additionally, include copies of vaccination records, as they may be required for accessing certain services or facilities.

Legal documents play a critical role in protecting your rights and assets. Ensure that you have copies of wills, power of attorney documents, and any legal agreements or contracts. These documents can be crucial in making decisions if someone is incapacitated or in managing the estate of a deceased family member. In the event of a disaster, having these legal records readily available can facilitate smoother transitions and legal proceedings.

Insurance policies are another must-have in your emergency document collection. Compile copies of all insurance policies, including health, home, auto, and life insurance. These documents will be necessary for filing claims and accessing benefits. Make a list of policy numbers, coverage details, and contact information for your insurance agents. Keeping these documents organized can expedite the claims process and ensure you receive the support you need.

Educational records should not be overlooked, especially if you have children. Include copies of school transcripts, diplomas, and standardized test scores. If your children are displaced and need to enroll in a new school, these records will help ensure a smooth transition. For students with special education needs, include copies of Individualized Education Plans (IEPs) and any other relevant documentation.

In addition to these essential documents, consider including a detailed inventory of your home's contents. This inventory should list valuable items, such as electronics, jewelry, and furniture, along with their approximate value and purchase receipts if available. Photographs or video recordings of each room can also be incredibly useful for insurance claims. Regularly update this inventory to reflect new purchases or changes in your household's contents.

To organize your emergency documents effectively, use a systematic approach. Start by categorizing documents into groups, such as identification, financial, health, legal, insurance, and educational records. Use labeled folders or binders to keep each category separate and easily accessible. For added protection, place these folders in a waterproof and fireproof container. This ensures that your documents remain safe from physical damage during a disaster.

Digital copies of your emergency documents can provide an additional layer of security. Scan each document and save them on a password-protected flash drive or an encrypted cloud storage service. Ensure that you regularly update these digital copies to reflect any changes in your information. Having digital backups allows you to access your documents from any location, which can be especially useful if you are evacuated or unable to return home immediately.

Communication is key during emergencies, so include a list of important contact information in your emergency document kit. This list should feature phone numbers and email addresses for family members, close friends, neighbors, and out-of-town contacts. Additionally, include contact information for emergency services, such as local fire, police, and medical facilities. Having this information readily available can facilitate quick communication and coordination during a crisis.

Regularly review and update your emergency documents to ensure they remain current and accurate. Life events, such as births, deaths, marriages, and changes in employment, can necessitate updates to your records. Set a schedule to review your documents at least once a year, and make any necessary adjustments. This proactive approach ensures that your information is always up-to-date and ready for use.

Involving your entire household in the process of gathering and organizing emergency documents can foster a sense of preparedness and shared responsibility. Hold family meetings to discuss the importance of these documents and ensure that everyone knows where they are stored. Assign specific tasks to each family member, such as updating medical records or maintaining the home inventory. By working together, you can ensure that your household is fully prepared to face any emergency.

Consider creating a concise emergency information sheet summarizing essential details from your documents. This sheet can include crucial information such as medical conditions, emergency contacts, and insurance policy numbers. Keep a copy of this sheet in your wallet or purse, and distribute copies to each family member. In an emergency, this sheet can provide quick access to vital information when you may not have time to search through your entire document kit.

Maintaining a well-organized collection of emergency documents and records is a cornerstone of disaster preparedness. By systematically gathering, organizing, and updating these documents, you can ensure that you are ready to handle any emergency with confidence and efficiency. This proactive approach not only protects your household's well-being but also provides peace of mind, knowing that you have taken the necessary steps to safeguard your essential information.

Long-Term Food Storage Solutions

When planning for long-term food storage, the goal is to ensure that you and your family have a reliable supply of nutritious food in case of emergencies. This involves selecting the right foods, storing them properly, and periodically rotating your stock to maintain freshness. A well-thought-out food storage plan can provide peace of mind and security, knowing that you are prepared to sustain yourself through unforeseen circumstances.

Start by choosing foods that have a long shelf life and require minimal preparation. Staples like rice, beans, pasta, and grains are excellent choices due to their durability and nutritional value. These items can be the backbone of your food storage plan, providing essential carbohydrates and proteins. Consider adding canned goods, such as vegetables, fruits, meats, and soups, which can last for years if stored properly. Canned foods are convenient because they are ready to eat and often contain valuable nutrients.

Dried foods are another important component of long-term food storage. Dried fruits, vegetables, and meats can be stored for extended periods and retain much of their nutritional content. Dehydrated meals, which are often used by campers and hikers, can also be a practical addition. These meals are lightweight, require only water to prepare, and offer a balanced diet in a compact form. Ensure that you include a variety of flavors and types to prevent menu fatigue and maintain morale during prolonged reliance on stored food.

Freeze-dried foods are a bit more expensive but offer the longest shelf life, often up to 25 years. These foods retain most of their original taste and nutrients because the freeze-drying process removes moisture while preserving the food's structure. Popular freeze-dried options include fruits, vegetables, meat, and complete meals. Because they require only water to rehydrate, they are convenient and easy to prepare even in challenging conditions.

Proper storage conditions are crucial for maintaining the quality of your long-term food supplies. The key factors are temperature, light, moisture, and air. Aim to store your food in a cool, dark, and dry place with a consistent temperature. Basements, pantries, and dedicated food storage rooms are ideal locations. Avoid areas that are prone to temperature fluctuations, such as garages or attics, as these can accelerate the degradation of food.

Containers play a significant role in protecting your food from environmental factors. Use food-grade containers that are airtight and moisture-resistant. Mylar bags, when used with oxygen absorbers, are excellent for storing dry goods like grains and beans. These bags can be sealed with heat to create a barrier against air and moisture. For added protection, place the Mylar bags inside sturdy plastic buckets with tight-fitting lids. Canning jars are another option for storing dried foods and can be vacuum-sealed to extend their shelf life.

Labeling is an often-overlooked aspect of food storage but is essential for effective management. Clearly label each container with the contents and the date of storage. This practice allows you to track the age of your supplies and ensures that you use the oldest items first, a method known as first-in, first-out (FIFO). Regularly inspecting and rotating your stock helps maintain its quality and prevents waste.

Beyond basic staples, consider including food items that cater to specific dietary needs and preferences. If any family members have allergies or dietary restrictions, ensure that your storage plan accommodates those needs. Gluten-free grains, lactose-free milk substitutes, and low-sodium options are readily available and should be part of your inventory if required. Additionally, comfort foods like chocolate, coffee, and spices can significantly improve morale during stressful times.

Water is a critical component of long-term food storage, as most stored foods will require water for preparation. Calculate the amount of water needed for both drinking and food preparation, and store an adequate supply. The general guideline is one gallon of water per person per day. Store water in food-grade containers, and consider including water purification tablets or a filtration system in case your water supply is compromised.

Maintaining a balanced diet is essential for health and well-being, even during emergencies. Diversify your food storage to include a mix of macronutrients and micronutrients. Protein can come from canned meats, beans, and legumes, while carbohydrates can be sourced from grains and pasta. Fats are also important and can be stored in the form of cooking oils, nuts, and seeds. Including a variety of fruits and vegetables ensures that you get necessary vitamins and minerals. Multivitamins can also be a valuable addition to your storage plan to compensate for any dietary gaps.

Planning for long-term food storage also involves considering the shelf life of different items. While some foods can last for decades, others have a shorter lifespan and need more frequent rotation. For example, white rice can last up to 30 years when stored properly, whereas brown rice, due to its higher oil content, has a shelf life of about six months to a year. Similarly, canned goods typically last between two to five years, depending on the type and storage conditions. Regularly checking expiration dates and consuming items before they spoil is crucial for maintaining a viable food supply.

In addition to food, consider including basic cooking and preparation tools in your storage plan. A manual can opener, portable stove, and fuel, along with basic utensils and cookware, ensure that you can prepare meals even if utilities are unavailable. Solar ovens and rocket stoves are alternative cooking methods that do not rely on traditional fuel sources and can be valuable in a prolonged emergency.

Building a long-term food storage plan is an ongoing process that requires regular assessment and adjustment. Start with a goal of accumulating a few weeks' worth of supplies and gradually expand to several months or even a year. Periodically review your inventory, update your stock, and refine your storage methods. Engaging your family in the planning process can help ensure that everyone understands the importance of preparedness and contributes to maintaining the food supply.

Incorporating these strategies into your long-term food storage plan ensures that you are prepared to sustain yourself and your loved ones through emergencies. By carefully selecting and storing a variety of foods, maintaining proper storage conditions, and regularly rotating your stock, you can build a resilient food supply that offers nutritional balance and peace of mind. This proactive approach to food storage not only provides security but also fosters a sense of preparedness and self-reliance in the face of uncertainty.

Access to clean, safe drinking water is a fundamental necessity, especially during emergencies when regular water supplies may be disrupted or contaminated. Understanding various water purification methods is crucial for ensuring that your household remains hydrated and healthy in any situation. This chapter explores different techniques to purify water, providing practical guidance on how to implement these methods effectively.

One of the most straightforward and widely practiced methods of water purification is boiling. Boiling water for at least one minute (or three minutes at higher altitudes) kills most pathogens, including bacteria, viruses, and parasites. This method is effective and requires minimal equipment—just a heat source and a pot. However, boiling does not remove chemical contaminants or sediments, so it's best used when biological contamination is the primary concern.

Filtration is another essential technique for purifying water. Water filters come in various types, including mechanical, activated carbon, and ceramic filters. Mechanical filters use physical barriers, such as fibrous or membrane materials, to remove particles and pathogens from water. These filters are rated by the size of particles they can remove, with smaller micron ratings indicating finer filtration. Activated carbon filters absorb impurities, including chlorine, volatile organic compounds (VOCs), and some heavy metals, improving the taste and smell of water. Ceramic filters have tiny pores that block bacteria and protozoa but may not be effective against viruses unless combined with other purification methods.

Portable water filters, such as those used by hikers and campers, are convenient for emergency situations. These filters are compact, lightweight, and can be used directly at the water source. Pump filters, gravity filters, and straw filters are common types. Pump filters require manual operation to push water through the filter, while gravity filters use the force of gravity to draw water through the filtration medium. Straw filters allow you to drink directly from a water source, filtering the water as you sip. While portable filters are highly effective for removing biological contaminants, they may not address all chemical pollutants, so it's important to choose a filter appropriate for your specific needs.

Chemical disinfection is another method to purify water, using substances like iodine, chlorine, or chlorine dioxide. These chemicals are effective against bacteria, viruses, and some protozoa. Iodine tablets or solutions can disinfect water in about 30 minutes, though the taste may be unpleasant, and they are not recommended for long-term use due to potential health risks. Chlorine bleach can also be used, with a typical dosage of 8 drops per gallon for clear water and 16 drops per gallon for cloudy water, followed by a 30-minute waiting period. Chlorine dioxide is available in tablet or liquid form and is effective against a wider range of pathogens, including Cryptosporidium, which is resistant to iodine and chlorine.

Ultraviolet (UV) light purification is a modern and highly effective method for disinfecting water. UV light disrupts the DNA of microorganisms, rendering them unable to reproduce and cause illness. Portable UV purifiers are available, often resembling a pen that you stir in the water for a specified duration. While UV purification is effective against bacteria, viruses, and protozoa, it does not remove chemical contaminants or sediments. Therefore, it's often used in conjunction with filtration to ensure comprehensive water treatment.

Distillation is a more complex but thorough method of water purification. This process involves boiling water to create steam, which is then condensed back into liquid form in a separate container. Distillation removes a wide range of contaminants, including bacteria, viruses, protozoa, heavy metals, salts, and many chemicals. However, it can be time-consuming and requires a significant amount of energy, making it less practical for large-scale or emergency use unless you have access to a reliable power source.

Solar disinfection (SODIS) is an accessible and low-cost method suitable for small-scale water purification. This technique involves filling clear plastic bottles with water and exposing them to direct sunlight for at least six hours. The combined effects of UV radiation and heat from the sun kill most pathogens. SODIS is particularly useful in regions with ample sunlight and limited resources, though it is less effective in cloudy conditions and does not remove chemical contaminants.

In emergencies where you need to purify water quickly and have limited resources, improvised methods can be lifesaving. One such method is using improvised charcoal filters made by layering charcoal, sand, and gravel in a container. Water is poured through these layers, which help to remove some impurities and improve the taste. While not as effective as commercial filters, this method can be useful when no other options are available. Always follow up with boiling or chemical disinfection to ensure the water is safe to drink.

Understanding the source and type of contamination is crucial when choosing a water purification method. Surface water from rivers, lakes, and streams is more likely to be contaminated with biological pathogens, while groundwater from wells may contain chemical pollutants. Urban water sources can have a mix of both. Testing your water for specific contaminants can help determine the most appropriate purification method. Home water testing kits are available and can identify common pollutants such as bacteria, nitrates, lead, and pesticides.

Maintaining your water purification equipment is essential for ensuring its continued effectiveness. Follow the manufacturer's instructions for cleaning and replacing filter elements, and store chemical disinfectants in a cool, dry place to prevent degradation. Regularly inspect your equipment for signs of wear or damage and replace components as needed. Proper maintenance not only extends the life of your equipment but also ensures that your water remains safe to drink.

Creating a water purification plan tailored to your household's needs involves considering factors such as the number of people, potential water sources, and the types of contaminants you might encounter. Store a variety of purification tools and supplies to ensure you can address different situations. For example, keep a combination of portable filters, chemical disinfectants, and a UV purifier in your emergency kit. Educate all family members on how to use each method and practice regularly to ensure everyone is familiar with the process.

By integrating these methods into your preparedness strategy, you can ensure a reliable supply of clean, safe drinking water in any emergency. Equipping yourself with the knowledge and tools to purify water effectively not only safeguards your health but also provides peace of mind. Whether you are facing a natural disaster, a temporary disruption, or a long-term crisis, having the ability to produce potable water is invaluable. This proactive approach to water purification enhances your resilience and self-reliance, empowering you to navigate any situation with confidence.

Cooking without power might seem daunting at first, but with some creativity and resourcefulness, it's entirely possible to prepare delicious and nutritious meals even during power outages or in remote locations. Whether you're dealing with an emergency situation or simply enjoying the great outdoors, understanding how to cook without conventional appliances is a valuable skill.

During a power outage, one of the most accessible tools for cooking is a propane or butane camp stove. These portable stoves are compact, easy to use, and provide a reliable heat source. Setting up a camp stove is straightforward: connect the fuel canister, light the burner, and adjust the flame to your desired level. Camp stoves can accommodate a variety of cookware, from small pots to larger pans, making them versatile for different types of meals. Always ensure you use these stoves in a well-ventilated area to avoid the risk of carbon monoxide poisoning.

Another effective method for cooking without power is using a charcoal grill. Charcoal grills are excellent for grilling meats, vegetables, and even baking bread. To start, arrange the charcoal briquettes in a pyramid shape and use lighter fluid or a chimney starter to ignite them. Once the coals are covered with white ash, spread them out evenly and place your food on the grill. The key to successful grilling is controlling the heat by adjusting the vents and arranging the coals for direct or indirect cooking. Direct cooking is ideal for steaks and burgers, while indirect cooking works well for larger cuts of meat and whole poultry.

Wood-fired cooking is another traditional method that can be highly effective. If you have access to a fire pit or a safe outdoor space for a campfire, you can use wood to cook your meals. Building a fire requires dry wood, kindling, and tinder. Arrange the tinder and kindling in a teepee shape, light it, and gradually add larger pieces of wood to build a steady flame. Once you have a good bed of hot coals, you can cook directly over the fire using a grill grate or cast-iron cookware. Cooking over an open flame adds a distinct smoky flavor to food, enhancing the overall taste.

Solar ovens are an innovative and eco-friendly option for cooking without power, especially on sunny days. A solar oven uses reflective materials to concentrate sunlight onto a cooking chamber, trapping heat and cooking food slowly. To use a solar oven, place it in direct sunlight and adjust the reflectors to maximize the amount of light entering the chamber. Solar ovens are ideal for baking, slow-cooking stews, and even dehydrating fruits. They are safe to use, as there are no flames or hot surfaces, making them a great option for families with children.

For those who prefer a hands-off approach, thermal cookers are a fantastic solution. A thermal cooker consists of an inner pot and an insulated outer container. To use it, bring your ingredients to a boil in the inner pot, then place the pot into the insulated container and seal it. The retained heat continues to cook the food slowly over several hours. This method is energy-efficient and retains the nutrients and flavors of the ingredients. Thermal cookers are excellent for soups, stews, and rice dishes.

Dutch ovens are versatile and durable, making them perfect for cooking without power. These heavy cast-iron pots can be used on a camp stove, over a charcoal grill, or directly in a campfire. Dutch ovens distribute heat evenly and retain it well, allowing you to bake, roast, and simmer with ease. For baking, place hot coals on the lid to create an oven-like environment. From baking bread to making hearty stews, Dutch ovens can handle a wide range of recipes.

If you're in a situation where you need to conserve fuel or lack conventional cooking tools, no-cook meals can be a lifesaver. These meals rely on ingredients that require no cooking, such as canned goods, dried fruits, nuts, and ready-to-eat foods. Combining canned beans with fresh vegetables and a simple dressing can create a nutritious salad. Wraps and sandwiches using canned tuna, chicken, or hummus are also quick and satisfying options. No-cook meals are not only convenient but also minimize cleanup and preparation time.

Harnessing the power of fermentation can also provide a means of preparing food without cooking. Fermented foods like sauerkraut, kimchi, and yogurt can be made with simple ingredients and time. These foods not only offer a way to preserve ingredients but also provide beneficial probiotics that support gut health. Fermentation requires a bit of patience, as the process can take days to weeks, but the results are rewarding and flavorful.

In addition to these methods, proper food storage and preparation are crucial when cooking without power. Keep a well-stocked pantry with non-perishable items such as canned vegetables, beans, pasta, rice, and grains. Store food in airtight containers to prevent spoilage and contamination. If you have access to a cooler or ice chest, use it to keep perishable items fresh for as long as possible. Plan your meals in advance to make the most of your available ingredients and minimize waste.

Learning to cook without power also involves mastering basic cooking techniques that don't rely on modern appliances. Knife skills, for example, become even more important when you can't rely on food processors or blenders. Practice chopping, dicing, and slicing to prepare ingredients efficiently. Understanding how to marinate and tenderize meats can enhance flavor and texture, even when you're limited to basic cooking methods.

Embrace the opportunity to explore new flavors and cuisines that are well-suited to cooking without power. Many traditional dishes from around the world are designed to be cooked with minimal equipment and resources. For instance, Middle Eastern mezze platters, Mexican tacos, and Southeast Asian salads often rely on fresh, raw ingredients and simple preparations. Experimenting with these cuisines can expand your culinary repertoire and make cooking without power an enjoyable and enriching experience.

Cooking without power requires adaptability and a willingness to experiment with different methods and techniques. With the right tools and mindset, you can create satisfying meals that nourish and comfort, even in challenging circumstances. By preparing in advance and honing your skills, you'll be well-equipped to handle any situation with confidence and creativity. Whether you're facing a temporary power outage or embarking on an outdoor adventure, the ability to cook without conventional appliances is a valuable and empowering skill that connects you to the timeless art of preparing food.

Understanding and meeting nutritional needs during a crisis is vital for maintaining health and energy levels, especially when regular food sources may be disrupted or unavailable. Crises can take many forms, from natural disasters and prolonged power outages to pandemics and economic downturns. In such times, ensuring that you have access to a balanced diet can help you stay resilient and better equipped to handle the challenges that arise.

The first priority during a crisis is to ensure you have a sufficient supply of water. Hydration is paramount, as the body can't survive more than a few days without water. Aim to store at least one gallon of water per person per day for drinking and sanitation purposes. If storing large quantities isn't feasible, consider having water purification tablets or a portable water filter on hand to make local water sources safe for consumption. Dehydration can quickly lead to severe health issues, so always prioritize clean drinking water.

When it comes to food, focus on non-perishable items that have a long shelf life and are easy to store. Canned goods, dried foods, and vacuum-sealed packages are excellent choices. These items not only last longer but are also less likely to spoil if refrigeration is lost. Canned vegetables, beans, and meats provide essential nutrients and can be combined to create balanced meals. Dried foods such as pasta, rice, lentils, and oats are versatile staples that can be the base for numerous dishes.

Protein is a critical component of your diet, especially during a crisis when physical and mental stress can be heightened. Look for sources of protein that are shelf-stable and easy to prepare. Canned fish like tuna or salmon, canned chicken, and legumes such as beans and lentils are all excellent options. Nut butters, like peanut or almond butter, are also nutrient-dense and have a long shelf life. These protein sources help repair tissues, maintain muscle mass, and support immune function.

Carbohydrates provide the energy necessary to keep you active and alert. Stock up on items like rice, pasta, quinoa, and oats, which can be stored for long periods without refrigeration. These foods are not only filling but also versatile, allowing you to create a variety of meals. Whole grains are particularly beneficial as they release energy more slowly, helping to maintain blood sugar levels and keep you feeling full longer.

Fats are another essential part of your diet, providing a concentrated source of energy and aiding in the absorption of fat-soluble vitamins (A, D, E, and K). Healthy fats can be found in items such as nuts, seeds, and oils. Olive oil and coconut oil are great choices as they have a longer shelf life compared to other types of fats. Including sources of omega-3 fatty acids, like flaxseeds or chia seeds, can also support brain health and reduce inflammation.

Vitamins and minerals are necessary for maintaining overall health and supporting immune function. During a crisis, fresh produce might be scarce, so consider stocking up on multivitamins to ensure you get the necessary nutrients. However, canned fruits and vegetables can still provide valuable vitamins and minerals. Opt for those without added sugars or salt when possible. Dried fruits are another good option, offering a concentrated source of vitamins and minerals along with fiber.

Fiber is important for digestive health and can be found in whole grains, beans, lentils, and dried fruits. Incorporating these foods into your diet can help maintain regular bowel movements and prevent digestive issues that might be exacerbated by stress and changes in routine.

In addition to selecting the right foods, consider how you will prepare them. Cooking fuel, such as propane or butane, and portable stoves should be part of your emergency supplies. If you have access to an outdoor space, a charcoal or gas grill can also be useful. Knowing how to cook with minimal equipment and ingredients is a valuable skill that can make a significant difference during a crisis.

Meal planning can help you use your supplies efficiently and ensure that you're getting a balanced diet. Plan meals that incorporate a variety of nutrients and rotate your stockpile to use items before they expire. Simple recipes that combine proteins, carbohydrates, and fats can be both nutritious and satisfying. For example, a meal of canned beans with rice and a drizzle of olive oil covers multiple nutritional bases.

Mental health is also a critical consideration during a crisis, and nutrition plays a role in maintaining it. Eating a balanced diet can help stabilize mood and energy levels. Comfort foods, while often less nutritious, can provide psychological relief and a sense of normalcy. Balance comfort foods with nutrient-dense options to support both physical and mental health.

It's also important to consider the needs of specific populations, such as children, pregnant women, the elderly, and those with chronic illnesses. These groups may have additional nutritional requirements that need to be planned for. For instance, children need more protein and fats relative to their size to support growth and development, while the elderly might need more calcium and vitamin D to maintain bone health.

Incorporating variety into your emergency food supplies can prevent food fatigue, where the monotony of eating the same foods repeatedly diminishes appetite and enjoyment. Spices, herbs, and condiments can add flavor and make meals more palatable. Consider stocking up on items like salt, pepper, garlic powder, and dried herbs, which can greatly enhance the taste of your meals.

In summary, meeting your nutritional needs during a crisis involves careful planning and preparation. Focus on storing a variety of non-perishable foods that provide proteins, carbohydrates, fats, vitamins, and minerals. Ensure access to clean drinking water and have a method for cooking your food. By maintaining a balanced diet, you can support your physical health, boost your immune system, and maintain the energy needed to navigate challenging circumstances. Preparing for specific dietary needs and incorporating a variety of flavors can also enhance your resilience and well-being during a crisis.

The first step to growing your own Growing and preserving food is a fundamental skill that not only enhances self-sufficiency but also ensures a steady supply of nutritious ingredients, particularly during uncertain times. Starting a garden and learning preservation techniques can seem daunting, but with practical steps and a bit of patience, anyone can cultivate and maintain a productive garden along with a well-stocked pantry.

food is choosing the right location. Ideally, select a spot that receives at least six hours of sunlight a day and has good drainage. If space is limited, container gardening can be a viable alternative. Raised beds are another excellent option, particularly if the soil quality in your area is poor. They provide better control over soil composition and drainage, and they can be built to a convenient height for easy access.

Once you've identified the location, it's time to prepare the soil. Healthy soil is the cornerstone of a productive garden. Begin by testing the soil's pH and nutrient levels, which can be done with a simple soil test kit available at garden centers. Based on the results, amend the soil with organic matter such as compost, which enriches it with essential nutrients and improves its structure. Composting kitchen scraps and yard waste is an eco-friendly way to create your own nutrient-rich soil amendment.

Selecting the right crops is crucial for a successful garden. Consider your local climate and growing season when choosing what to plant. Cool-season crops like lettuce, spinach, and radishes can be planted in early spring or fall, while warm-season crops such as tomatoes, peppers, and cucumbers thrive in the summer. It's beneficial to choose a mix of quick-growing vegetables and those that take longer to mature, ensuring a steady harvest throughout the growing season. Heirloom varieties are particularly valuable as they are often more resilient and flavorful.

Starting seeds indoors can give your garden a head start. By planting seeds in trays or pots a few weeks before the last expected frost, you can transplant healthy seedlings into the garden once the weather warms up. This method is especially useful for crops with long growing seasons. Be sure to harden off seedlings by gradually exposing them to outdoor conditions to prevent transplant shock.

Companion planting is a technique that involves growing certain plants together to enhance growth, deter pests, and improve yields. For example, planting basil alongside tomatoes can enhance flavor and repel insects, while marigolds can deter nematodes in the soil. Intercropping, which involves planting different crops in the same space, can also maximize use of space and reduce weed competition. Corn, beans, and squash, known as the "Three Sisters," are a traditional intercropping trio that benefits each other in various ways.

Watering your garden properly is essential. Overwatering can lead to root rot, while underwatering can stress plants and reduce yields. Aim to water deeply and less frequently rather than shallow and often, encouraging roots to grow deeper. Mulching with straw, leaves, or grass clippings helps retain moisture, suppress weeds, and regulate soil temperature.

As your garden begins to thrive, it's important to monitor for pests and diseases. Regularly inspect plants for signs of trouble, such as holes in leaves, discoloration, or wilting. Integrated pest management (IPM) is an effective approach that combines different strategies to control pests with minimal environmental impact. This might include introducing beneficial insects like ladybugs, using organic pesticides, and practicing crop rotation to prevent soil-borne diseases.

Harvesting at the right time ensures that your produce is at its peak flavor and nutritional value. Each crop has its own indicators for ripeness; for instance, tomatoes should be fully colored but still firm, while cucumbers are best picked before they become too large and seedy. Gentle handling during harvest prevents damage and extends the shelf life of your produce.

Preserving the bounty from your garden allows you to enjoy homegrown food year-round. There are several preservation methods to consider, each suitable for different types of produce. Canning is a popular method that involves processing fruits, vegetables, and even meats in jars at high temperatures to kill bacteria and create a vacuum seal. Pressure canning is necessary for low-acid foods like green beans and meats, while water bath canning works for high-acid foods like tomatoes and pickles.

Freezing is another straightforward preservation method. Blanching vegetables before freezing helps preserve their color, texture, and nutritional value. Simply boil vegetables for a few minutes, then plunge them into ice water to stop the cooking process before packing them into freezer bags or containers. Fruits can be frozen directly or after being prepared into purees or jams.

Dehydrating removes moisture from food, inhibiting the growth of bacteria and mold. This method is particularly useful for fruits, vegetables, and herbs. Dehydrators provide a controlled environment for drying, but you can also use an oven set to a low temperature or even air dry certain items. Properly dried foods should be crisp or leathery and can be stored in airtight containers for long periods.

Fermentation is an age-old preservation technique that not only extends shelf life but also enhances the nutritional value of food. Fermented foods like sauerkraut, kimchi, and yogurt are rich in probiotics, which support gut health. Fermentation involves submerging vegetables in a brine solution and allowing beneficial bacteria to convert sugars into acids, creating a tangy, preserved product.

Pickling is another method that uses vinegar or brine to preserve vegetables and fruits. The acidity from the vinegar prevents spoilage and adds a distinct flavor. Quick pickling involves submerging produce in a hot vinegar solution and refrigerating it, while traditional pickling requires a fermentation period at room temperature before storage.

Proper storage of preserved foods is crucial to ensure their longevity. Store canned goods in a cool, dark place to prevent spoilage, and regularly check seals to ensure they remain intact. Frozen foods should be kept at 0°F (-18°C) or lower to maintain quality, and be sure to label packages with dates to use the oldest items first. Dried foods should be stored in airtight containers away from light and moisture to prevent rehydration and spoilage.

Growing and preserving your own food is not only a practical skill but also a rewarding experience that connects you to the cycles of nature and the origins of your food. It requires effort and dedication, but the benefits of fresh, homegrown produce and the security of a well-stocked pantry are well worth it. By learning and practicing these techniques, you can enjoy the flavors and nutritional benefits of your garden's bounty throughout the year, enhancing your resilience and self-sufficiency in the process.

Reinforcing Your Home

Ensuring your home is adequately reinforced can make a significant difference in your safety and peace of mind, particularly during emergencies or natural disasters. Whether you are preparing for severe weather, potential intrusions, or other unforeseen events, reinforcing your home involves a series of practical steps that enhance its structural integrity and security.

To begin with, assess the existing condition of your home. Walk around the exterior and interior, taking note of any visible weaknesses or areas that require attention. Look for cracks in the foundation, gaps around windows and doors, and any signs of wear and tear on the roof. Identifying these issues early allows you to prioritize repairs and reinforcements more effectively.

Strengthening the foundation is critical, as it supports the entire structure of the house. If you notice any cracks or settling, consult with a structural engineer to determine the best course of action. In some cases, you might need to add piers or underpinning to stabilize the foundation. Regularly checking for water pooling around the base of your home and ensuring proper drainage can help prevent further foundation problems.

The roof is another crucial component to reinforce. A sturdy roof not only protects against rain and wind but also provides insulation. Inspect your roof for missing or damaged shingles, and replace them promptly. Consider installing hurricane straps or clips to secure the roof to the walls, which can significantly reduce the risk of it being blown off during high winds. Additionally, ensure your attic is well-ventilated to prevent moisture buildup, which can weaken the roof over time.

Windows and doors are common entry points for both weather and intruders. Reinforcing them is essential for enhancing your home's security. Start by installing impact-resistant windows or applying shatter-resistant film to existing windows. This can prevent glass from shattering during storms or break-ins. For added protection, consider adding storm shutters that can be quickly deployed when needed.

Doors should be solid and equipped with high-quality locks. Reinforce door frames with longer screws and metal strike plates to make them harder to kick in. Installing a deadbolt lock provides an additional layer of security. For sliding doors, place a metal rod or wooden dowel in the track to prevent them from being forced open. Peepholes or security cameras at entry points allow you to see who is outside before opening the door.

Garages are often overlooked but can be vulnerable points of entry. Ensure your garage door is reinforced with braces and that it has a secure locking mechanism. If your garage is attached to your home, make sure the door leading into the house is as secure as your main entry doors. Installing motion sensor lights around the garage can also deter potential intruders.

Beyond physical reinforcements, consider improving your home's overall security system. Install a comprehensive alarm system that includes sensors on doors and windows, motion detectors, and surveillance cameras. Many modern systems offer remote monitoring via smartphone apps, allowing you to keep an eye on your property even when you are away.

Lighting plays a significant role in home security. Well-lit exteriors can deter intruders by eliminating hiding spots. Install motion-activated lights around the perimeter of your home, particularly near entry points and dark corners. Inside, use timers on lights to give the appearance that someone is home, even when you are not. This simple measure can dissuade would-be burglars.

In addition to lighting, landscaping can also impact your home's security. Keep shrubs and trees trimmed away from windows and doors to eliminate potential hiding spots. If you have a fence, ensure it is in good repair and consider adding locks to gates. Thorny bushes planted under windows can provide a natural deterrent to intruders.

Water damage can be as devastating as any other threat. Protecting your home from flooding involves several proactive measures. Start by ensuring that your gutters and downspouts are clean and in good working order, directing water away from your foundation. Installing a sump pump in your basement can help manage groundwater and prevent flooding. It's also wise to grade the land around your home so that water flows away from the foundation rather than pooling next to it.

If you live in an area prone to earthquakes, additional reinforcements are necessary. Secure heavy furniture and appliances to walls to prevent them from toppling over during tremors. Install flexible gas lines to reduce the risk of gas leaks and fires. Reinforce the walls and roof to withstand seismic activity, and consider adding bracing to the foundation to improve stability.

Fire safety is another critical aspect of home reinforcement. Install smoke detectors in every room and test them regularly to ensure they are functioning properly. Keep fire extinguishers in key areas like the kitchen and garage, and make sure all household members know how to use them. Creating and practicing a fire escape plan can save lives in the event of an emergency.

Incorporating these reinforcements not only protects your home but also enhances its value and longevity. By taking a proactive approach to home reinforcement, you can mitigate risks and create a safer living environment for you and your family. Each step, from securing the foundation to installing a comprehensive security system, contributes to a holistic strategy that addresses various potential threats.

Bear in mind that reinforcing your home is an ongoing process. Regular maintenance and updates are necessary to keep your home in optimal condition. Stay informed about new technologies and methods that can further enhance your home's safety and security. Investing time and resources into these measures provides peace of mind, knowing that your home is well-protected against a range of potential dangers.

Ultimately, a well-reinforced home is a testament to your commitment to safety and preparedness. It reflects a proactive stance in safeguarding your most valuable asset and ensuring the well-being of those who reside within it. By diligently applying these principles and techniques, you can create a resilient and secure home that stands up to the challenges of time and nature.

Fire Safety Measures

Fire safety measures are essential to protect your home and loved ones from the devastating effects of a fire. Implementing these measures involves a combination of preventive actions, proper equipment, and emergency planning. By understanding the risks and taking proactive steps, you can significantly reduce the likelihood of a fire and ensure everyone knows what to do if one occurs.

The first line of defense against fire is prevention. Many household fires start in the kitchen, so it is crucial to exercise caution while cooking. Never leave cooking food unattended, and keep flammable items, such as dish towels and paper towels, away from the stove. Regularly clean your oven and stovetop to prevent grease buildup, which can ignite easily. Using a timer can help you remember when to check on food in the oven or on the stove.

Electrical safety is another key aspect of fire prevention. Regularly inspect electrical cords and replace any that are frayed or damaged. Avoid overloading electrical outlets and use surge protectors to safeguard your appliances. If you notice flickering lights, a burning smell, or sparking outlets, these could be signs of electrical issues that need immediate attention from a qualified electrician. Be mindful of the placement of electrical cords and ensure they are not pinched under furniture or rugs, which can cause wear and overheating.

Heating equipment, such as space heaters, fireplaces, and wood stoves, also pose fire risks. Keep anything that can burn at least three feet away from heating equipment. Use space heaters with automatic shut-off features and place them on a stable, non-flammable surface. Have your chimney inspected and cleaned annually to prevent the buildup of creosote, a highly flammable substance that can cause chimney fires. Additionally, ensure portable heaters and fireplaces are turned off and extinguished when you leave the room or go to bed.

Proper installation and maintenance of smoke alarms are critical for early fire detection. Install smoke alarms on every level of your home, inside bedrooms, and outside sleeping areas. Test them monthly to ensure they are working correctly and replace the batteries at least once a year. Consider interconnected smoke alarms, so when one alarm sounds, they all do, providing an earlier warning. Replace smoke alarms every ten years or as recommended by the manufacturer.

Carbon monoxide detectors are equally important, especially if you use gas appliances, fireplaces, or have an attached garage. Carbon monoxide is an odorless, colorless gas that can be deadly. Install detectors outside sleeping areas and on every level of your home. Test them regularly and replace batteries as needed. Knowing the symptoms of carbon monoxide poisoning, such as headache, dizziness, and nausea, can help you act quickly if a detector goes off.

Fire extinguishers provide a crucial tool for combating small fires before they spread. Place extinguishers in key areas like the kitchen, garage, and near any heating equipment. Ensure everyone in the household knows how to use an extinguisher properly, following the PASS method: Pull the pin, Aim the nozzle at the base of the fire, Squeeze the handle, and Sweep from side to side. Regularly check the pressure gauge and replace or service extinguishers as needed.

Creating and practicing a fire escape plan can save lives in the event of a fire. Start by drawing a floor plan of your home, marking all exits, including windows and doors. Identify two ways out of every room if possible. Designate a meeting place outside the home where everyone will gather. Practice the escape plan with all household members, including children and pets, at least twice a year. During drills, teach everyone to stay low to the ground to avoid smoke inhalation and to check doors for heat before opening them.

In addition to a fire escape plan, teach your family basic fire safety rules. Emphasize the importance of not using elevators during a fire and the need to call 911 from a safe location. Ensure everyone knows how to stop, drop, and roll if their clothing catches fire. Familiarize children with the sound of smoke alarms so they are not frightened and know to respond quickly.

Proper storage of flammable materials can prevent accidental fires. Store gasoline, paint, and other flammable liquids in approved containers and keep them in a well-ventilated area, away from heat sources. Avoid storing these materials in living spaces or near exits. Keep matches and lighters out of reach of children, and educate them about the dangers of playing with fire.

Maintaining a clean and clutter-free home reduces fire hazards. Regularly discard old newspapers, magazines, and other combustible materials that can accumulate. Keep your yard free of dry leaves, branches, and other debris that can fuel a fire. If you have a fireplace, store ashes in a metal container and dispose of them properly.

In areas prone to wildfires, additional precautions are necessary. Create a defensible space around your home by clearing vegetation and other flammable materials within at least 30 feet of the structure. Use fire-resistant landscaping materials and plant fire-resistant shrubs and trees. Keep gutters and roofs clear of leaves and other debris that can ignite from embers. Consider installing spark arresters on chimneys to prevent sparks from escaping.

Community involvement can enhance fire safety for everyone. Participate in local fire safety programs and encourage neighbors to adopt similar precautions. Share your fire escape plan with friends and family, and offer to help them create their own. Supporting local fire departments through donations or volunteer work can also contribute to overall community safety.

Staying informed about fire safety trends and new technologies can further protect your home. Advances in fire detection and suppression systems, such as smart smoke alarms and home sprinkler systems, offer additional layers of protection. Regularly review and update your fire safety measures to ensure they remain effective and aligned with current best practices.

By integrating these fire safety measures into your daily routine, you can create a safer environment for yourself and your family. Fire prevention, early detection, and a well-practiced escape plan are the cornerstones of a comprehensive fire safety strategy. Taking the time to implement these measures not only protects your home and belongings but also provides peace of mind, knowing you are prepared for any fire-related emergencies that may arise.

Prepping your home to withstand floods and earthquakes requires a multi-faceted approach that combines structural modifications, landscape adjustments, and emergency planning. Understanding the unique challenges posed by these natural disasters can help you implement effective strategies to protect your property and ensure the safety of your family.

Floodproofing begins with assessing your home's vulnerability to water damage. If your property is in a flood-prone area, elevating the structure above the base flood elevation is a critical measure. This can be done by raising the foundation on piers, stilts, or concrete blocks, creating space for floodwaters to flow beneath the house. For homes that cannot be elevated, wet floodproofing methods, such as installing flood vents in foundation walls, allow water to enter and exit the basement or crawl space, reducing the risk of structural damage.

Sealing your home against water intrusion is another essential step. Apply waterproof coatings and sealants to the exterior walls, foundation, and basement floors to prevent seepage. Installing sump pumps with battery backup systems in basements can help manage water that does penetrate, effectively reducing the risk of flooding inside. Ensure that your property has proper drainage systems, including gutters, downspouts, and French drains, to direct water away from your home's foundation.

Landscaping plays a significant role in flood prevention. Grading your yard to slope away from the house can prevent water from pooling around the foundation. Planting native vegetation and installing rain gardens can absorb excess rainwater, reducing runoff. Additionally, permeable paving materials for driveways and walkways allow water to infiltrate the ground rather than running off into storm drains, which can become overwhelmed during heavy rains.

Protecting utilities and major appliances is crucial in floodproofing your home. Elevate HVAC systems, water heaters, and electrical panels above the potential flood level. Consider relocating these systems to higher floors if possible. Installing backflow preventers on sewer lines can prevent sewage from backing up into your home during flooding events. For added protection, store important documents and valuables in waterproof containers or on upper levels of the house.

Earthquake proofing requires reinforcing the structural integrity of your home to withstand seismic activity. Start by securing heavy furniture, appliances, and electronics to walls using brackets and straps. This prevents them from toppling over and causing injuries or further damage during an earthquake. Anchoring large items such as bookcases and water heaters can also prevent gas leaks and fires.

Strengthening the foundation and framing of your home is vital in earthquake-prone areas. Retrofitting older homes with foundation bolts and braces can enhance their stability. This involves attaching the wooden frame to the concrete foundation with metal bolts and using plywood or steel plates to reinforce cripple walls. Consulting a structural engineer can help determine the best retrofitting methods for your specific home.

Flexible connections for gas and water lines can prevent leaks and ruptures caused by ground movement. Installing automatic gas shutoff valves that activate during an earthquake can mitigate the risk of gas-related fires. Reinforcing chimneys with plywood or metal straps can prevent them from collapsing and causing additional damage.

Creating a defensible space around your home can reduce earthquake damage. Remove dead trees, overhanging branches, and any other hazards that could fall on your house during a quake. Secure outdoor items such as patio furniture, grills, and garden tools to prevent them from becoming projectiles.

Emergency planning is a crucial component of flood and earthquake preparedness. Develop a family emergency plan that includes evacuation routes, communication strategies, and a designated meeting place. Ensure all family members know how to turn off utilities, including gas, water, and electricity, in case of an emergency. Assembling an emergency kit with essentials such as water, non-perishable food, medications, flashlights, and first aid supplies can sustain your family during the initial aftermath o a disaster.

Stay informed about the risks in your area. Local government websites, weather services, and emergency management agencies often provide valuable information on flood zones and earthquake hazards. Signing up for emergency alerts can keep you updated on imminent threats, allowing you to take timely action.

Insurance is an important consideration for homeowners in flood and earthquake-prone areas. Standard homeowners' insurance policies typically do not cover damage from floods or earthquakes, so purchasing additional coverage is essential. Flood insurance can be obtained through the National Flood Insurance Program (NFIP), and earthquake insurance is available through private insurers or state programs in high-risk areas. Reviewing your insurance policies regularly ensures you have adequate coverage for rebuilding and repairs after a disaster.

Community involvement can enhance your preparedness efforts. Joining or forming a neighborhood emergency response team can provide mutual support during and after a disaster. Sharing resources, skills, and information with neighbors can strengthen overall resilience. Participating in local drills and training sessions can improve your readiness and help you stay calm and effective in an actual emergency.

Retrofitting your home for flood and earthquake resistance is an investment in safety and peace of mind. While some measures may seem costly, the potential savings in avoided damage and the protection of your family's well-being are invaluable. Regular maintenance and updates to your flood and earthquake-proofing strategies ensure they remain effective as conditions and technologies evolve.

By taking these proactive steps, you can significantly reduce the impact of floods and earthquakes on your home and family. The combination of structural modifications, landscape adjustments, and emergency planning creates a comprehensive approach to disaster preparedness. This holistic strategy not only safeguards your property but also enhances your ability to respond and recover from natural disasters, ensuring a safer future for you and your loved ones.

Home Security Systems

Securing your home involves more than just locking doors and windows; it requires a comprehensive approach that integrates technology, strategic planning, and vigilant habits. Home security systems have evolved significantly over the years, providing advanced protection against break-ins, theft, and other intrusions. Understanding how to effectively utilize these systems can give you peace of mind and ensure the safety of your loved ones and belongings.

Modern home security systems typically consist of various components that work together to create a robust defense. These include alarm systems, surveillance cameras, motion detectors, smart locks, and more. Each element serves a specific purpose, and when combined, they offer comprehensive coverage. Choosing the right components for your home depends on your specific needs and the layout of your property.

Alarm systems are the cornerstone of most home security setups. They act as a first line of defense, alerting you and the authorities to any unauthorized entry. When selecting an alarm system, consider one with a loud siren and a reliable notification system, such as text alerts or automated calls. Many modern alarm systems are connected to professional monitoring services, which can dispatch emergency responders when an alarm is triggered. This added layer of protection ensures a swift response even if you're not at home.

Surveillance cameras have become increasingly accessible and affordable, making them a popular choice for home security. Strategically placed cameras can deter potential intruders and provide valuable evidence in the event of a break-in. High-definition cameras with night vision capabilities ensure clear footage around the clock. Position cameras to cover all entry points, including doors, windows, and driveways. Consider installing both visible and hidden cameras; the visible ones act as a deterrent, while the hidden ones can capture activity if the visible ones are tampered with.

Motion detectors are another crucial component of a home security system. These devices sense movement within a specified area and trigger alarms or lights when activity is detected. Place motion detectors in high-traffic areas such as hallways, staircases, and near entrances. Advanced motion detectors can differentiate between humans and pets, reducing the likelihood of false alarms. Integrating motion detectors with your alarm and lighting systems can create an effective deterrent, startling intruders and alerting you to their presence.

Smart locks offer a convenient and secure way to control access to your home. These locks can be operated remotely via smartphone apps, allowing you to lock and unlock doors from anywhere. They also provide the ability to create temporary access codes for guests, service providers, or family members, which can be revoked once they're no longer needed. Some smart locks also integrate with other smart home devices, enabling you to create automated routines, such as unlocking the door when you arrive home and locking it when you leave.

In addition to these technological solutions, reinforcing physical barriers is essential for home security. Ensure all doors and windows are made of sturdy materials and equipped with high-quality locks. Deadbolts provide extra security for exterior doors, while window bars or security film can prevent easy access through windows. Sliding doors are particularly vulnerable, so install additional locks and place a rod or dowel in the track to prevent them from being forced open.

Lighting plays a significant role in deterring potential intruders. Well-lit exteriors make it difficult for burglars to approach your home unnoticed. Install motion-activated lights around the perimeter of your property, especially near entry points. These lights not only startle intruders but also make it easier for you and your neighbors to spot suspicious activity. Indoor lighting can also be used strategically; set timers to turn lights on and off, giving the impression that someone is home even when the house is empty.

While technology and physical barriers are vital, developing good security habits is equally important. Always lock doors and windows, even when you're at home. Avoid hiding spare keys in obvious places like under the doormat or in a flowerpot; instead, give a spare key to a trusted neighbor or friend. When leaving for an extended period, notify a neighbor or ask someone to check on your home regularly. This not only deters burglars but also ensures any issues like a broken window or water leak are addressed promptly.

Community involvement can enhance your home security efforts. Join or start a neighborhood watch program, where residents work together to keep an eye on each other's properties and report suspicious activity. Sharing information about recent incidents and security tips can help everyone stay vigilant and informed. Strong community ties create a network of support, making it more difficult for criminals to operate unnoticed.

Emergency preparedness is another aspect of home security that shouldn't be overlooked. Create an emergency plan for your family, including evacuation routes and a designated meeting place. Ensure everyone knows how to use the security system and what to do if an alarm is triggered. Regularly review and practice your emergency plan to keep it fresh in everyone's minds.

Insurance is an important consideration in your overall security strategy. Homeowners' insurance can provide financial protection in the event of a break-in or property damage. Review your policy to understand what is covered and consider additional coverage if necessary. Some insurance companies offer discounts for homes equipped with security systems, providing an added incentive to invest in these measures.

Staying informed about the latest security trends and technologies can help you maintain an effective defense. Advances in smart home technology, such as integrated security systems that connect to your smartphone or voice assistants, offer new ways to enhance your home's protection. Regularly updating your security system and software ensures you're protected against new threats and vulnerabilities.

In conclusion, securing your home requires a multi-layered approach that combines technology, physical barriers, good habits, and community involvement. By investing in a comprehensive home security system and adopting vigilant practices, you can significantly reduce the risk of break-ins and ensure the safety of your family and property. Taking these proactive steps not only deters potential intruders but also provides peace of mind, knowing you've done everything possible to protect your home.

Designing a safe room in your home is a critical step toward ensuring the safety of your family during emergencies such as natural disasters, home invasions, or other unforeseen events. A safe room, also known as a panic room, provides a secure space where you can retreat and wait for help or ride out a crisis. This chapter will guide you through the essential considerations and steps for creating a safe room that meets your specific needs and provides peace of mind.

The first aspect to consider when planning a safe room is its location within your home. Ideally, the safe room should be easily accessible from the main living areas but discreet enough to avoid detection by intruders. Common locations for safe rooms include basements, closets, or interior rooms without windows. Basements are particularly advantageous in areas prone to tornadoes or hurricanes due to their lower elevation and sturdy construction. However, if flooding is a concern, an above-ground interior room might be more appropriate.

Once you've chosen a location, the next step is to reinforce the room structurally. The walls, ceiling, and floor of the safe room should be fortified to withstand significant force. Reinforcement can be achieved by using materials such as steel, concrete, or Kevlar. For existing rooms, adding steel plates or reinforcing with concrete can enhance their resilience. The door to the safe room is equally important; it should be made of heavy-duty steel or solid wood and equipped with high-security locks and deadbolts. A reinforced door frame and hinges will further prevent forced entry.

Ventilation is another crucial consideration. A safe room should have a reliable air supply to ensure that occupants can breathe comfortably for extended periods. This can be achieved through dedicated air vents with filter systems that protect against smoke, gas, or other contaminants. In some cases, an independent air filtration system might be necessary, especially if the safe room is intended to protect against chemical or biological threats.

Equipping your safe room with essential supplies is vital for ensuring that you can remain safe and comfortable until help arrives. Stock the room with non-perishable food, bottled water, a first aid kit, flashlights, batteries, blankets, and basic hygiene products. A battery-operated or hand-crank radio can keep you informed about the outside situation. Additionally, consider including a charging station for cell phones and other critical electronic devices. If space allows, a small portable toilet can provide added comfort during extended stays.

Communication is key during any emergency, so ensure that your safe room has the means to contact the outside world. A landline phone, if feasible, provides a reliable communication method that doesn't rely on battery power. However, cell phones and two-way radios are also essential, as they offer portability and additional communication options. Ensure that these devices are fully charged and have backup power sources available.

Security features such as surveillance cameras, peepholes, or intercom systems can enhance the functionality of your safe room. Surveillance cameras placed inside and outside the room allow you to monitor the situation without exposing yourself to danger. Peepholes or small windows with one-way glass can serve a similar purpose, providing visibility while maintaining security. An intercom system can facilitate communication with family members or emergency responders outside the room.

Training and preparedness are fundamental to making the most of your safe room. All family members should be familiar with the location, access procedures, and operation of the safe room. Conduct regular drills to ensure that everyone knows how to quickly and efficiently reach the safe room in various scenarios. These drills should cover different types of emergencies, such as break-ins, natural disasters, or fires, and emphasize the importance of staying calm and following the plan.

In addition to physical preparations, mental readiness is crucial for effectively using your safe room. Encourage open discussions among family members about the importance of the safe room and the various situations in which it might be used. Address any fears or concerns and provide reassurance that the safe room is a tool designed to protect them. Building this understanding and confidence will help everyone respond more effectively in an actual emergency.

Considerations for specific threats can further tailor your safe room to your needs. For example, in areas prone to tornadoes, the safe room should be designed to withstand high winds and flying debris. This might include reinforced walls and a solid roof structure. For home invasions, soundproofing the room can prevent intruders from hearing occupants, and concealment features such as hidden entrances can enhance security. In regions where earthquakes are a concern, ensuring that the room is resistant to structural collapse and has secure storage for emergency supplies is essential.

Legal and insurance considerations are also part of the planning process. Check local building codes and regulations to ensure that your safe room complies with all requirements. Some areas may have specific standards for storm shelters or panic rooms, and adherence to these standards can improve the room's effectiveness and your peace of mind. Additionally, inform your insurance provider about the safe room, as it may affect your coverage or qualify you for discounts.

The process of creating a safe room involves both initial investment and ongoing maintenance. Regularly inspect the room and its features to ensure that they remain in good working order. Replace expired supplies, check the functionality of communication devices, and test the security systems periodically. Keeping the safe room in a state of readiness ensures that it will perform as expected when needed.

In conclusion, a well-designed safe room is a vital component of a comprehensive home security strategy. By carefully selecting the location, reinforcing the structure, equipping it with essential supplies, and ensuring effective communication and security features, you can create a space that offers protection and peace of mind during emergencies. Training and preparedness further enhance the effectiveness of your safe room, ensuring that your family is ready to respond swiftly and calmly in any situation. Investing in a safe room is not just about physical safety; it's about providing a haven where your family can feel secure and protected in the face of uncertainty.